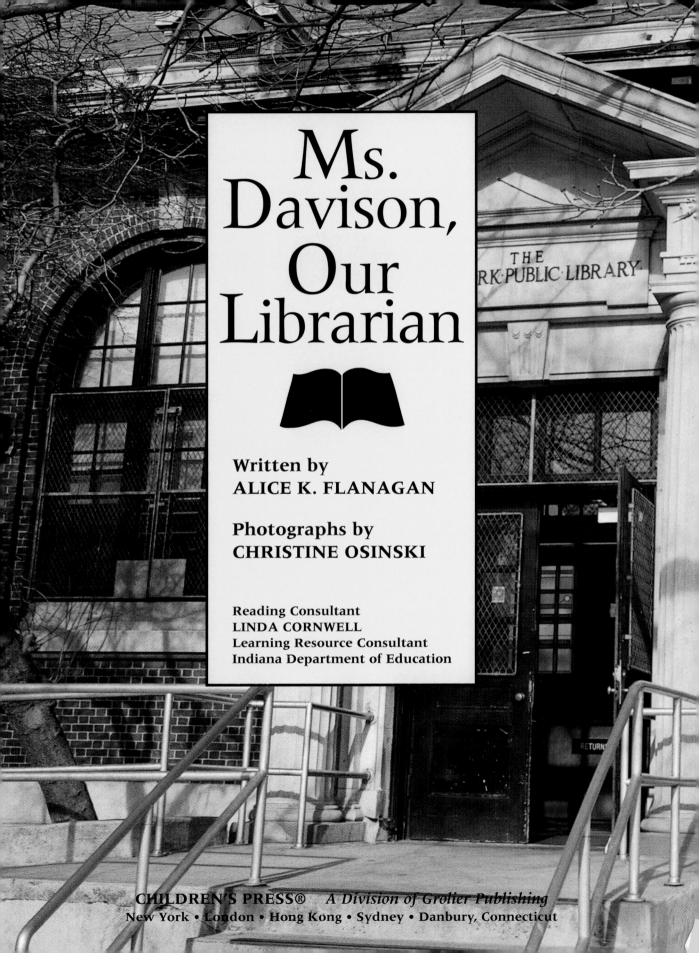

Ms. Davison, Our Librarian

Written by
ALICE K. FLANAGAN

Photographs by
CHRISTINE OSINSKI

Reading Consultant
LINDA CORNWELL
Learning Resource Consultant
Indiana Department of Education

CHILDREN'S PRESS® *A Division of Grolier Publishing*
New York • London • Hong Kong • Sydney • Danbury, Connecticut

Special thanks to Dorothy Davison for allowing us to tell her story.

Also, thanks to the St. George Library Center of the New York Public Library.

Library of Congress Cataloging-in-Publication Data
Flanagan, Alice.
    Ms. Davison, our librarian / by Alice K. Flanagan; photographs by Christine Osinski.
    p. cm. — (Our neighborhood)
    Summary: Simple text and photographs describe the duties and responsibilities of a public librarian who helps people access information.
    ISBN 0-516-20009-7 (lib. bdg.) — 0-516-26060-X (pbk.)
    1. Libraries—Juvenile literature.   2. Librarians—Juvenile literature.
[1. Librarians. 2. Occupations. 3. Libraries.] I. Osinski, Christine, ill.
II. Title.
    Z665.5.F58   1996
    020'.92—dc20   96-17166
                                                                    CIP
                                                                    AC

Photographs ©: Christine Osinski

Whenever I go to the library,

I see Ms. Davison, our librarian.

She helps me find
what I want to know—

what life was like long ago,

how machines are made,
and why planes fly,

who is famous now,
where animals live,

A New True Book

SQUIRRELS

what the world was like
when I was born.

Ms. Davison knows
just where to look—

in a computer,
on a CD-ROM,

in newspapers,

or in a book.

She works with information
all day long.

She makes it available
to everyone—

the young,

the old,

even those with special needs.
This boy reads Braille with his
fingers because he cannot see.

When the sick and elderly
can't get to the library,
Ms. Davison brings the library to them.

19

Being a librarian is a busy job.

There are books, and videos,
and audiocassettes to order.

All items are checked before they
leave the library and when they
come back again.

They all must be returned
to their proper places.

Ever since Ms. Davison was
a little girl, books have been her
favorite things.

Now she works in a library
near the neighborhood
where she grew up.

26

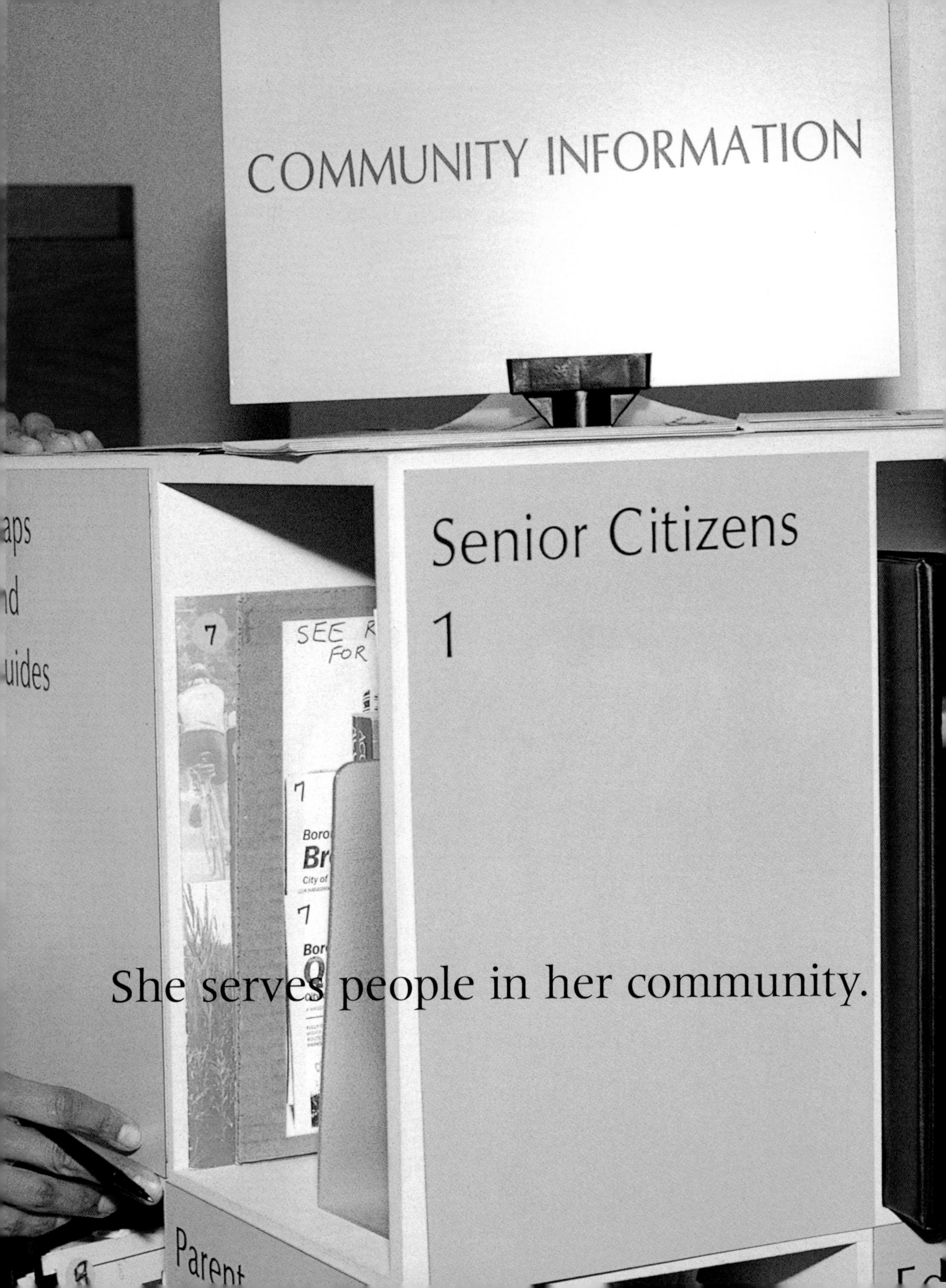

COMMUNITY INFORMATION

...aps
...nd
...uides

Senior Citizens
1

7

SEE R
FOR

7

Bor
Br
City of

7

Bor
9
O

She serves people in her community.

Parent

8

Ms. Davison is intelligent
and patient.

With her help, people learn
about the present and the past.

Brian Lanker
EAM A WORLD
Portraits of Black Women Who Changed America
THURGOOD MARSHALL
TONI MORRISON
WORTH
ROBERT
OPPENHEIMER
JESSE OWENS
SATCHEL
Behrman
FERRIS
LUIS J. RODRIGUEZ
ALWAYS RUNNING
Cwiklik
Sequoyah AND THE CHEROKEE ALPHABET
DENMARK VESEY
Malone
Barbara Walters
Edwards
THEO AND ME
GREAT LIVES
LECH WALESA
BY REBECCA STEFOFF
MELTZER
GEORGE WASHINGTON And the
WALTER WHITE
MALCOLM X
MAKE IT PLAIN
FOR BEGINNERS
OSCAR WILDE
YA

Together they shape future dreams by reading and remembering all they can.

31

Meet the Author
and the Photographer

Alice Flanagan and Christine Osinski are sisters. They grew up together telling stories and drawing pictures in a brown brick bungalow in a southwest-side neighborhood of Chicago, Illinois. Today they write stories and take photographs professionally.

Ms. Flanagan resides in Chicago with her husband and works as a freelance writer. Ms. Osinski is a photographer and teaches at The Cooper Union for the Advancement of Science and Art in New York City. She lives with her husband and two sons on Staten Island.